British Native Trees
Their Past and Present Uses

British Native Trees

Their Past and Present Uses

Including a guide to
burning wood in the home

Piers Warren

Published by

Wildeye
United Kingdom

Email: info@wildeye.co.uk
Websites: www.wildeye.co.uk/trees
            www.wildeye.co.uk/publishing

Many thanks to Roland Clare for editing.

Contents

Introduction

Years ago when I was a tree surgeon in Norfolk I became fascinated with native trees and the variety of uses to which they have been put in the past. I was struck by the sheer diversity of uses, knowledge of which must have been handed down and built on, generation after generation. I found myself wondering how the more obscure uses were discovered – often by necessity and trial and error I expect. I got a real feeling for how tough life was for some of our ancestors, and yet also a feeling of warmth, simplicity and of the value of well-crafted items that is difficult to recreate these days.

I find that the uses of native trees today can be split into five categories:

1. Those that will never be needed again, such as the use of elm underbark to make gruel.

2. Those that continue to decline such as the use of lime for piano parts.

3. Those which have been rekindled, such as the production of charcoal from coppice woods, even if only for the leisure market of barbecues, and the production of beautiful furniture.

4. Continuing industries such as the use of oak and beech by hardwood sawmills.

5. New uses such as the willow sound barriers, and the use of birch in cancer treatments.

In the last few decades the knowledge of traditional tree importance has been lost, and we can see this echoed in the tropical rainforests where the local tribes, with their accumulated skills, are being forced out of the forests. Thankfully in the Western World we have books as a permanent record of some of this knowledge, but this is not so in the rainforests where much of it is lost. In just the last decade or so there has been a growing revival of interest in some of the 'nearly lost' crafts, and it is good to see newcomers taking up bodging, charcoal making, and coppicing, even if only on a tiny scale compared to a century or two ago.

I mainly deal with the uses of native tree *products* – my study does not include the many, and very important uses of *living* native trees. These include amenity and landscaping uses, shelter for stock and crops, sporting and recreation, waste-land reclamation, wildlife habitats and so on. By *products* I mean principally the wood, but also the bark, roots, sap, leaves and fruit where particular uses have been made of them.

To determine the 35 native species (divided into 21 genera) I have followed the late Alan Mitchell – former British tree guru and author of the *Collins Field Guide to the Trees of Britain and Northern Europe*. There is also the question of what is a tree and what is a bush? There are definitions such as diameter of stem, but this doesn't always help – hazel for example is most commonly found as a hedge plant or coppiced to grow rods of narrow diameter. Yet if hazel is allowed to grow naturally it will form a small tree. Again I have followed Alan Mitchell's categorisation.

For each genus (group of related species) I start with a

general description of the wood, followed by a variety of the traditional uses, and finally the current (and possible future) uses. The lists are by no means exhaustive – any native wood may have been used to make a spoon or a toy or a tool at some time by our ancestors – the aim being to show the diversity of uses, and those to which certain genera are most suitable. With a few exceptions I have not looked too deeply at the medicinal uses of native trees (worth a separate project in its own right), and have deliberately not got bogged down in the bulk markets of modern commercial timber production.

Although demand for wood is growing (it has doubled since 1950), domestic supply has not increased to meet this demand, and now only 12% of our requirements is grown in the UK. The result is mass importing of timber – some of which comes from unsustainable markets. If imported wood becomes scarce and more expensive, then wooden products will become dearer and the demand for them will fall.

Although there is some resurgence of interest in, and desire for, native wood products such as furniture, these are now expensive due to the scarcity of trees and craftsmen. There are currently only 1,500 wood craftsmen in Britain, using some 10,000 cubic metres of hardwood timber per year. The most productive native species still in regular demand these days are oak and beech (the bread-and-butter timber of hardwood sawmills), Scots pine, ash and cherry (for their excellent timber) and birch (for timber and firewood).

I think that it's sad that many people today cannot recognise native trees, and do not realise how vital they were to our ancestors. In these disposable-days of plastics and metals where the priorities are cheapness and convenience, there is little perceived need for native trees. The result is their decline at the expense of wildlife, the environment, and maybe our souls. A beautiful cherry-wood cabinet or a set of bowls turned in apple-wood are more valuable (in terms other than financial) than a snap-together cupboard and bulk-made crockery!

Coppicing

This is the technique originating from Neolithic times of regularly cutting trees just above ground level, resulting in the growth of a number of roughly-equal straight branches. These can be put to many uses – to make hay-rakes, hurdles, barrel hoops for example. A key aspect of this technique is that it is a sustainable management, and has been used for many native tree species, although not all regenerate well from the stools (stumps left at ground level).

The length of time between cutting the poles varies from a few years to 25 years depending on the species and the intended use. Ash for walking sticks will be cut every 4–7 years for example, and birch for broom handles every 10–15 years. Coppicing can also greatly increase the life of individual trees – some ancient hazel stools in England are estimated to be over 1,500 years old. In earlier times coppicing was of great importance, providing the raw materials for many large-scale industries, but since the mid-nineteenth century it has declined. Today there are only a few scattered coppice men left working in the UK, mainly producing craft items, but there does seem to be a renewed interest in the technique.

Pollarding is a similar method to coppicing, except the trees are cut at a height of 2-3m, beyond the reach of deer and stock who would eat the young shoots. It is also practised in city streets to stop the trees growing too large whilst keeping low branches away from pedestrians and traffic.

Charcoal Production

Charcoal has been produced in the UK for at least 4,500 years, and was once far more widespread than it is today, when only a few specialists remain practising the technique. Charcoal burners were often found in or near coppice woods as their raw materials were the coppice poles of various native trees – oak, ash, birch and alder still being used today.

Production involves the slow burning of wood with a restricted supply of oxygen. In the past this was done by building piles of poles, covering with leaves and earth, and then lighting a fire in the middle – although more recently large iron kilns were used. Great care has to be taken to ensure the wood does not burn too quickly and produce ash – this is done by controlling the flow of air through vents around the sides of the pile or kiln.

Up to the Second World War charcoal was a vital source of fuel for many industrial processes, but it has largely been superseded by oil. These days the biggest market for charcoal in the UK is for barbecue fuel, yet only 3% of UK charcoal consumption is produced in this country. A third of our charcoal comes from South East Asian mangrove forests, half of which have been destroyed over the last fifty years as a result. This is a tragedy, especially considering that there is enough coppice woodland in South East England alone to supply the whole of the UK barbecue market with a superior product. Attempts are being made to promote the use of UK-produced charcoal, but there is a long way to go.

Firewood

Wood is the natural sustainable choice of fuel for domestic fires – in use since the first fire many millennia ago. When we warm our homes with wood, we participate in a natural cycle and an ongoing continuum of activity that we share with ancient ancestors. I am amazed at the number of country people who don't have fires, whether open log fires or woodburning stoves, because they are "too dirty" or "too much work". In fact the procedure of building and lighting the fire is one of my favourite jobs of the day, and I love handling and preparing the firewood. I am not one to pursue a life where all comfort comes from the flick of a switch.

Wood fuelled the open fires of the hunter-gatherers, the brick ovens of the first bakers, and, until the 19th century, all homes. We love to sit in front of a fire and watch its magical flames speak to us and warm our souls. Have you noticed that when the TV is switched off everyone stares at the fire? And watching a fire is certainly far more relaxing than watching TV! Fires inspire intimate conversation. When we come in from the cold, we are drawn to the fire. No other fuel is as alive.

The ability to burn wood for heat in your home gives you more freedom and options for fuel. You are no longer dependent on large energy utilities and multinational corporations who may or may not be able to supply power and fuel. Even if you have to buy in your logs at least you are supporting your local economy. But what are the environmental implications of burning wood?

Environmental Issues

When we burn wood we are releasing solar energy, in the form of heat, that has been stored in the wood as chemical energy. The process of photosynthesis converted solar energy, water and carbon dioxide into oxygen and the organic molecules that form the wood, half the weight of which is carbon. So burning wood is just the quick reversal of this process, liberating the sun's heat when we need it most.

Unlike the burning of fossil fuels like coal, gas or oil, burning firewood releases no more greenhouse gases (carbon dioxide) than would be produced were the wood to simply rot on the forest floor. If we are responsible in the ways we grow, cut, and burn our firewood, wood burning can actually be a good choice for the environment.

Note that I mention 'grow' our firewood – for of course this must be done sustainably. There are many parts of the world where forests are disappearing as growing populations collect daily firewood without planting new trees. This is avoidable – wood is a renewable resource, which means that it can be replenished by nature in a period of time that is compatible with our human use. Provided they are cared for and managed properly, our forests can be a perpetual source of fuel, unlike gas, oil, and coal, which we are being depleted at a rate far faster than the millions of years it took nature to make them. On the smallholding it is up to us always to plant more trees than we cut down, and if we buy logs from a wood merchant, to make sure they come from a sustainable source.

So burning wood is a good choice from the greenhouse gas point of view but what about other pollution – surely all that smoke can't be good? Smouldering, smoky fires that produce a plume of blue-grey smoke from the chimney are the main cause of wood heat-related air pollution. Smoke is made up of many tiny airborne particles and wood smoke can be harmful when it is inhaled. In some countries wood smoke has become a major air pollution problem and this has led to both local regulations and more efficient wood-burning appliances.

One thing to make clear at this stage is that if you are burning the right wood in the right way then there shouldn't be much smoke. As you probably know from bonfires, a slow, wet fire produces lots of thick smoke – in the fireplace we are aiming for a quick, hot, dry burn producing very little smoke. Another thing to bear in mind is that a smoky fire is an inefficient one – we want all the released energy to heat our home – not to go up the chimney in the form of complex particles. Carbon dioxide, the product of a clean, hot burn, is a colourless non-particulate gas, so a hot fire with minimal smoke is an efficient energy-converter with less pollution.

Sources of wood

There are two main choices – buy it in or grow your own. If buying from a log merchant you should expect to pay in the region of £40–£50 for good truck load – and I mean a heaped Transit load not a smaller pick-up. Ensure the logs are well seasoned and dry – I have in the past received logs described as 'seasoned' (in that they were chopped a year ago) but soaking wet from lying about in the rain for weeks!

When I say 'grow your own' I realise not everyone is lucky enough to have a small wood! I don't have a wood but I do have a lot of trees and hedges – and the prunings of these provide a large part of my fuel each year. Remember when it comes to pruning or felling you are often thinking a year ahead or more in terms of actually burning the wood, as it will need time to season.

Where I live, with no shortage of quiet country lanes, I often find large limbs blown off trees and lying in, or next to, the road. By taking these home for firewood I am doing the land-owners and road-users a favour – but do remember that this wood does belong to the landowner – so ask permission before helping yourself to logs on your Sunday afternoon walk through the neighbouring farmer's wood.

As I own a chainsaw and associated kit (helmet, visor, ear protection, gloves, protective trousers and lumberjack boots) I often get free firewood by helping neighbours. So ask those living around you if they have any dead trees, stumps, damaged branches etc that they want removed – in exchange for the wood. At this point I must say that using a chainsaw is a dangerous and skilled job – so make sure that you have appropriate training. Many agricultural colleges do short courses in chainsaw use which are well worthwhile. Any work with a chainsaw above ground (ie using a ladder or climbing with ropes in trees) should be undertaken only by a qualified tree surgeon, or if you have had the necessary training.

Which wood?

So what sort of wood burns best? Well there is an old anonymous poem which answers this very question:

LOGS TO BURN

Logs to burn, logs to burn,
Logs to save the coal a turn
Here's a word to make you wise,
When you hear the woodman's cries.
Never heed his usual tale,
That he has good logs for sale,
But read these lines and really learn,
the proper kind of logs to burn.

OAK logs will warm you well,
If they're old and dry.
LARCH logs of pine wood smell,
But the sparks will fly.
BEECH logs for Christmas time,
YEW logs heat well.
SCOTCH logs it is a crime,
For anyone to sell.

 BIRCH logs will burn too fast,
CHESTNUT scarce at all
HAWTHORN logs are good to last,
If you cut them in the fall
HOLLY logs will burn like wax
You should burn them green
ELM logs like smouldering flax
No flame to be seen

PEAR logs and APPLE logs,
they will scent your room.
CHERRY logs across the dogs,
Smell like flowers in bloom
But ASH logs, all smooth and grey,
burn them green or old;
Buy up all that come your way,
They're worth their weight in gold.

Note that all woods burn better when seasoned and some burn better when split rather than as whole logs. In general the better woods for burning that you are most likely to come by (including non-native species) are:

Apple and pear – burning slowly and steadily with little flame but good heat. The scent is also pleasing.

Ash – the best burning wood providing plenty of heat (will also burn green but you should not need to do this!)

Beech and hornbeam – good when well seasoned

Birch – good heat and a bright flame – burns quickly.

Blackthorn and hawthorn – very good – burn slowly but with good heat

Cherry – also burns slowly with good heat and a pleasant scent.

Cypress – burns well but fast when seasoned, and may spit

Hazel – good, but hazel has so many other uses hopefully you won't have to burn it!

Holly – good when well seasoned

Horse Chestnut – good flame and heating power but spits a lot.

Larch – fairly good for heat but crackles and spits

Maple – good.

Oak – very old dry seasoned oak is excellent, burning slowly with a good heat

Pine – burns well with a bright flame but crackles and spits

Poplar – avoid all poplar wood – it burns very slowly with little heat – which is why poplar is used to make matchsticks.

Willow – very good – in fact there is growing interest in biomass production of coppiced willow as a fuel.

Seasoning

So what is *seasoning*? Essentially it is making wood fit for burning – by reducing its water content – usually by leaving it for a period of time in the right conditions. All wood contains water. Freshly-cut wood can be up to 45% water, while well-seasoned firewood generally has a 20–25% moisture content. Well seasoned firewood is easier to light, produces more heat, and burns cleaner.

If you try to burn green wood, the heat produced by combustion must dry the wood before it will burn, using up a large percentage of the available energy in the process. This results in less heat delivered to your home, and gallons of acidic water in the form of creosote deposited in your chimney. This can eat through the chimney lining and cause significant damage. The problem is that as wet wood burns slowly, with little heat, the chimney flue does not get a chance to warm up. There is little draw (air moving up the chimney) which doesn't help the combustion, and the flue remains a cold surface on which the creosote condenses. Dry wood will burn hot – heating up the flue, creating a fast draw, and shooting the smaller amount of vapours out of the chimney before they get a chance to condense.

The first step to drive the water out of the wood is to cut it into lengths – let's say about 12–18 inches long (or less if your fireplace/woodburning stove requires this). Tree branches and trunks contain thousands of microscopic tubes which carry water from the roots to the leaves, and these tubes can stay full of water for years after the tree has been felled (or pruned). Cutting the wood to shorter lengths opens these tubes to the atmosphere which increases evaporation.

The second step is splitting any logs that are more than say six inches in diameter. This increases the surface area of the wood exposed to the elements and therefore also enhances drying. So the cutting and splitting of logs should be done as soon as possible after the wood is harvested – not just before you want to burn it. You can get mechanical splitters, and attachments for a tractor, when you have large quantities to split, but they are not cheap.

For the average user a maul is the tool needed. A maul is a type of axe with a heavy, wide head especially for splitting logs – you can buy one from a forestry supplier for about £40 new. A maul does not need to be particularly sharp – unlike a narrow felling axe which slices at wood and needs to be sharpened regularly. You *can* use a felling axe for splitting logs but it is much harder work than a maul. The trick with a maul is to let the weight of the head do the work – swing the maul over your shoulder and let the head fall on to the log without forcing it down. The wide head will force the log apart. It's also important to have the log you are splitting at a good height – on a tree stump or larger log about 18 inches to 2 feet off the ground is ideal – this makes the job easier and avoids back damage.

It takes a bit of practice to start with, but once you've 'got your eye in' you should be impressively splitting each log first time every hit – and be able to keep this up for a few hours at a time without feeling exhausted. It's a task I thoroughly enjoy – and have always referred to it as 'earning my cow pie'!

<u>Storing Firewood</u>

Once prepared the logs then need the proper storage to help them season properly. For most types of wood you should plan on at least six months' seasoning – some heavier woods like oak will need a year or more and all will benefit from longer. So at the least you should be cutting and splitting over winter, finishing by the end of March for use the following October onwards.

The first stage of seasoning involves using the sun and wind to help dry out the logs – so until the end of August the logs can be spread out in the open or stacked in rows. Then, before the weather turns they can stacked in your wood store to keep dry for use over the winter (or even the next winter after that). The aim of the wood store is to keep rain and snow off the logs, but still to allow maximum air circulation to aid the continual drying of the wood. So ideally a wood store will have a sloping roof but open sides. The bottom of the store should be old patio slabs or similar so the logs aren't resting on damp earth.

It is also vital to arrange your store so that you are using the most seasoned logs first. If you just have one compartment you will also be taking the top logs off the pile which have been put there most recently – and the old dry logs will sit at the bottom forever. It's the same principle as needing more than one  compost heap – one to add new material to, and another to rot down and use. So build two or more separated compartments in your store – or have two or more stores: one area for last year's logs that are ready to use, and one to add new logs to this year. Remember to plan the source of your wood far in advance – it really cannot be overemphasised that the key to a good fire is well-seasoned wood.

Of course it is a good idea to site your log store close to the house – so you don't have far to trudge to in the middle of the night when you need a few more logs. I also always keep as many logs as possible around the fire/stove. These have a final chance to dry and warm up before use. So each day the logs used to build the fire are ones that were well heated by last night's fire – then the stock is replenished for this night's. In an open fire you need to be quite sure these stored logs cannot be ignited. Before you go to bed always check that the fire is safe (or out) or close the doors of the woodburner.

Kindling

We must also mention kindling – an essential material to help start the log fire – for we must aim *never* to use 'firelighters'! When you are doing your pruning simply collect all the twiggy bits, cut or snap into useable lengths and store in cardboard boxes under cover. A few months is enough to dry kindling ready for use – but in practice it should be the twigs from last winter's pruning that are used as kindling this winter.

Don't forget that all sorts of other sources of kindling can be found – off-cuts from the carpentry workshop or sawmill for example, strips of bark, old broken bamboo canes, fences that have fallen apart, derelict sheds etc. It's all a form of recycling. Keep a box of kindling near to the fire/stove so it's crispy dry and ready for use the next night.

Building the fire

It's funny how some people have a knack for building a fire – the 'one-match-wonder' – but I would say that it is a skill that anyone can learn. It's a matter of having the right materials and common sense. Build it right and you should light a roaring blaze with one match and no firelighters every time.

The first technique to grasp is that of using layers of decreasing speed of combustability – i.e. paper lights quickly, burns fast but not for long, logs light and burn slowly, but once lit burn for a long time. When I build a fire I always aim for five layers:

1. **Paper** – old newspaper is great but you can also recycle junk mail and other used paper this way – screw the paper into balls (not too tightly) and make a layer at the bottom of the grate or woodburning stove.

2. **Cardboard** – tear off strips of old/damaged cardboard boxes, roll into tubes and place on the paper.

3. **Kindling** – place a good layer of kindling on top of the paper and cardboard – which will produce enough fast heat to get the kindling burning.

4. **Small logs** – a few small logs (say a couple of inches in diameter) will provide a stepping stone between the kindling and the larger log.

5. **Large logs** – finally add a couple of full-sized logs to the top of the pile. If you have some softwood logs (e.g. conifers) it would be good to start with these as they will get going faster than hardwood logs (e.g. oak). Be prepared to add a few more logs soon after these have got going.

Light the bottom paper with one match and sit back with your cuppa. This preparation may sound quite time-consuming but once you have a system – and materials to hand – it's really no problem at all. Certainly a lot easier than spending the next half hour on your hands and knees blowing furiously at a few smouldering sticks... .

TREES BY GENUS

Acer – Maple

Species: *Acer campestre* – field maple.

Wood Properties

Maple is a pale wood, often with beautiful veins and rippled grain. It can be worked very thin, making good veneers.

Past Uses

Maple was often sought after and used for high quality woodwork such as cabinets and musical instruments.

It was used to make the back, sides, neck and bridge of violins – the rippled grain used for the backs being known as 'fiddleback'.

In ancient times it was also used for the wooden parts of musical harps.

Maple was also grown in copses for firewood alongside other species such as hazel.

The bark is astringent – a decoction has been used to bathe sore eyes.

The sweet sap was used for making wine and syrup, and sugar could be extracted from the wood by boiling.

Maple syrup is still very popular, especially in Canada and America, as a pancake topping – but the syrup is largely made from Canadian maples.

Present Uses

Maple is rarely available in any size or quantity these days, but is popular for woodwork such as cabinets if it can be sourced.

The wood of maple roots is often knotted and is valued for small objects of cabinet work.

The leaves can be packed around apples, rootcrops etc to help preserve them over the winter. Field maple is a fast growing plant and as it bears clipping well it makes an excellent clipped hedge. It has also been used in topiary

(Sycamore (*Acer pseudoplatanus*), although not native, is an *Acer* that has been in the UK for some time (introduced from central Europe) and has been used for turning, carving and for making kitchen implements.)

Alnus – Alder

Species: *Alnus glutinosa* – alder

Wood Properties

Alder is a relatively soft, porous wood, which is not durable unless it is permanently under water. It is a pinky brown colour and can be used as a substitute for softwoods in the construction and repair of buildings. 'Scots Mahogany' is alder wood which has been immersed in peat bogs until the reddish stain it acquires as a result has become permanent.

Past Uses

With its durability underwater alder was often used in constructions such as pumps, piles, sluices, troughs, small boats and punts. River banks were strengthened with alder posts which often rooted – the root mats giving even more stability to the banks.

The bark was used for tanning (colouring leather), and when soaked with iron produced a black ink used for writing and as a dye for fabrics.

Tannic acid produced from alder bark was used by fishermen as a net-preservative. The dried bark (and leaves) also have medicinal properties due to their tannin and were used to treat colds and chills.

Until the early twentieth century alder was coppiced in North East England and Wales to provide the raw materials for clog sole cutter gangs. Clogs were a very common footwear with an alder sole and a leather upper, often worn by farm workers. Wearing clogs was compulsory in certain trades that involved standing on wet floors.

Before synthetic dyes started to come into general use, the alder gave us some of the finest dyes for wool and linen.

Green alder branches can make good whistles and panpipes, an important attribute for a tree to possess in the days before mass entertainment.

Alder also produced a superior gunpowder charcoal.

Present Uses

Alder has the right acoustic qualities for guitar necks and the bodies of electric guitars.

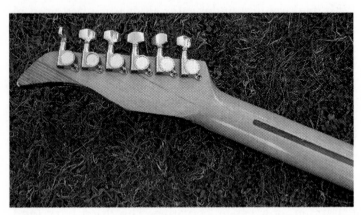

It is still coppiced and used to make charcoal on a small scale.

Alder can be used for turnery (it is sought after for its red colour which develops after cutting), and also to make pallets and as a source for pulpwood (timber stocks that are cut for paper production).

Arbutus – Strawberry Tree

Species: *Arbutus unedo* – strawberry tree/arbutus

Wood Properties

The wood of the evergreen strawberry tree is hard and dull brown with a fine pink grain. The bark has a dark reddish-brown colour.

Past Uses

The strawberry tree is so called because of the appearance of the fruit, but the Latin name 'unedo' means 'I eat one (only)' as the fruit is not very palatable. It does have a somewhat gritty skin, but the fruit itself has the texture of a lush tropical fruit. The fruit has been used to make delicious and nourishing jams and preserves. Birds do favour the raw fruit however and are responsible for spreading the seeds.

The bark was occasionally used for leather tanning.

Arbutus wood used to provide the prime charcoal for goldsmiths.

Present Uses

These days the wood of the strawberry tree is used only to make souvenirs at Killarney in Ireland – one of the few places where it grows wild. It is also known as the Irish strawberry tree or the Killarney strawberry.

In other European countries where the strawberry tree is more common a wine is made from the fruit, and a sugar and spirit have also been extracted from it. The young shoots of the tree are also recommended as winter food for goats and for making baskets.

Betula – Birch

Species: *Betula pendula* – silver birch
         Betula pubescens – downy birch

Wood Properties

Birch produces a hard, tough timber that is golden brown or white, and moderately dense.

Past Uses

Birch was used for small turned items such as tool handles, broom heads, furniture and toys.

It was also coppiced for charcoal production and to produce stems for making broom handles and bean poles.

Birch wood was favoured for smoking herrings and making herring barrels, butter-prints, bobbins, spools and reels.

The strong but flexible twigs were used to make besoms (the classic witch's brooms), as well as fire-beaters and steeplechase jumps.

Green birch poles were, until recently, used to stir molten copper in the refineries of Wales. This prevented oxides forming, resulting in purer copper.

The thin bark was used to make cups and ladles, and in the Middle Ages fishermen in Northumberland set light to strips of bark to attract fish to their spears at night.

The sweet sap from birch was used to make woodsman's tea, and evaporated to make a solid sugar – sold as a sweetmeat called maple sugar (despite not coming from maple!).

Oil from birch bark is an effective insect repellent.

Present Uses

A few birch besoms are still made today.

It is an excellent firewood and is also occasionally used to make fence posts.

Birch is commonly planted in Scotland where it is used to produce timber for turnery, furniture, pallets and pulpwood.

The sap is still tapped in spring to make birch sap wine in Inverness. Here the Frasers run a family business in their castle, producing 7,000 bottles of wine per year. The wine is made by mixing the birch sap with raisins, sugar, lemon juice and yeast and then fermenting as you would any country wine.

It has recently been discovered that birch bark contains chemical compounds that can slectively kill human cancer cells with no side effects. Compounds made from the bark  include butalin and betulinic acid, also called bet A.

Research is continuing for possible future use in this field.

Birch bark can also be used to treat skin conditions such as warts and eczema.

Carpinus – Hornbeam

Species: *Carpinus betulus* – hornbeam

Wood Properties

Hornbeam is one of the hardest woods and because of this is also known as 'ironwood'. It is creamy white in colour.

Past Uses

Hornbeam was used where hardness was required – for example the teeth of mill cogs, piano hammers, chopping blocks, workshop floors and ox-yokes.

It is an excellent firewood which is said to burn with the greatest heat and the brightest flame for the longest time. As a result it was sometimes known as 'candlewood', and used to provide artificial lighting so that cottage crafts could be practised in the evenings.

Present Uses

Hornbeam is not in much demand these days, except perhaps as a good firewood.

Small markets include high quality craft items, and occasionally it is used to make skittles and golf club heads.

A yellow dye can be obtained from the bark of the

hornbeam and used to colour woollen yarns and other materials.

Corylus – Hazel

Species: *Corylus avellana* – hazel   (although not considered as a tree by some, Alan Mitchell has given it 'the benefit of the doubt').

Wood Properties

Hazel is a hard, pale brown wood. It is one of the most commonly coppiced species, producing hard heavy sticks, and rods which can be split or twisted without breaking.

Past Uses

Coppiced hazel was traditionally very important and had many uses including being used for making thatching materials (liggers, spars, sways and pegs), hurdles for pens and animal traps and cages – such as pheasant traps and putchers (used for catching salmon).

The sticks were also used to make barrel hoops, dowsing rods, besom handles, and ships' fenders (as bundles of sticks tied together hung over the side of the ship to stop it bumping harbour walls when moored).

'Faggots' were bundles of hazel brushwood used in country kitchens to create a quick blaze when lighting the fire.

Hazel sticks were also the ideal wattle for wattle and

daub – used as the base of plaster walls in lowly houses.

Hazel charcoal was the favourite for making gunpowder when it was introduced to the West in the Middle Ages. Guns and bombs were first invented in the fourteenth century, and from then on increasing amounts of gunpowder were demanded. The traditional recipe was:

> 1 part charcoal (preferably hazel)
> 2 parts brimstone (sulphur)
> 6 parts saltpeter (potassium nitrate)

Wood from hazel roots was sought out for veneers, toys and fancy ware.

The nuts are edible and the shells were used as beads for necklaces.

Present Uses

A few coppices are still worked in southern England for items such as: thatching spars, hurdles, walking sticks, besom handles and tent pegs (which are in great demand by marquee firms, camping stores and the army).

Crataegus – Hawthorn

Species: *Crataegus monogyna* – hawthorn (quickthorn, whitethorn, or may)

Crataegus oxyacanthoides – Midland hawthorn

Wood Properties

Hawthorn is a pinky-brown wood that is hard and tough. It is fine-grained.

Past Uses

Hawthorn has been used to make hedging stakes, walking sticks, rake teeth, mallet heads, and the ribs of small boats.

The wood is a good fuel, and makes good charcoal.

Bundles of hawthorn branches were used to make 'brush barrows' – dragged across fields to break the soil over newly sown seed crops.

The haws (as the berries are called) were made into jellies, wines, liqueurs and ketchups.

Present Uses

Hawthorn is still used for fine work such as veneers, cabinets and fine boxes. It is also sought after for fine engraving (of woodblocks for printing for example).

(Hawthorn is most commonly used as a hedging plant, particularly in rural locations, but this falls outside the scope of this study).

Fagus – Beech

Species: *Fagus sylvatica* – beech

Wood Properties

Beech wood is heavy, strong, and white or pinky-brown with brown flecks. It is susceptible to insect attack and therefore not suitable for construction and rarely used outdoors. As the wood is clean and odourless it is good for kitchen fittings. It tends to split and distort when dried, but lasts well underwater.

Past Uses

Despite the fact that beech is one of the trees that does not coppice well, it has had many uses over the years including the following: bellows, boot-lasts (blocks of wood shaped like a human foot that boots are made on), butter-pats, bowls, fishing floats, oars, parquet flooring, pestles and mortars, granary shovels, clothes pegs, piano frames, rolling pins, saddle trees for saddlers and hat boxes.

Beech bends well with steam heat and as a result was often used to make curved chair backs and legs: this was known as 'bodging'. The craft of bodging has a history dating back at least five hundred years. The bodger was basically an itinerant woodland worker who specialised in making cheap, but high quality, legs, back spindles and stretchers for Windsor chairs.

It is unsure how bodgers got their name. It cannot come from derogatory term applied to a clumsy worker, 'a bodge job', as bodgers are a highly skilled craftsmen. It may derive from 'badger', the name once given to travelling salesmen, some of whom were bodgers. Alternatively, the term may come from the animal badger, as the men lived a life much like the badger, only seen at dawn and dusk entering or emerging from the wood, and spending the day deep amongst the trees.

The foundation piles under Winchester Cathedral and some of those under the old Waterloo Bridge were made of beech.

Cabinet makers used to blacken and polish beech wood to make it look like ebony. It was also treated with a mixture of soot and urine to give it the appearance of walnut, but this effect didn't last long.

Beech has been used for the high heels in women's shoes, and in the Second World War beech plywood was used in the construction of Mosquito bombers.

The earliest bound books were encased in thin beechwood sheets beneath leather covers, and early printers carved their fonts out of beech.

The wood burns fast and hot and was traditionally the fuel for bread ovens.

In the eighteenth and nineteenth centuries a potent liquor called 'noyau' was made out of beech leaves.

Beechnut oil has been used for cooking and the beechmast (or nuts) were eaten in times of famine.

Present Uses

Beech wood is in demand by sawmills as an all-purpose hardwood. It is used for furniture, flooring, mallet heads,  laminations, pallets, and pulpwood.

A few bodgers still practise their craft of making chairs from beech wood in the Chilterns.

It is a good wood for turnery – beech that has been invaded by fungus often produces attractive patterns when turned (known as 'dozed beech').

It is sometimes used for tool handles and sports equipment such as golf woods.

A liqueur can be made by steeping beech leaves in gin for a couple of weeks and then filtering before adding sugar. It's the same approach as for making sloe gin but produces a green liqueur.

Fraxinus – Ash

Species: *Fraxinus excelsior* – ash

Wood Properties

Ash is the toughest wood and can withstand pressure and shock with little risk of fracture.

Past Uses

With its toughness ash has been put to many uses including the following: tool handles, sports equipment (bats, racquets, hockey sticks etc), coach building, spears, pikes, arrows, wheelbarrows, parts of sailing boats, sledge runners, wheel rims, shepherds' crooks, feeding cribs, gymnasium woodwork, police truncheons, drum rims, hay rakes, and rungs for ships' rope-ladders.

Ash coppices well, the poles being cleft for fencing and other uses.

Its use in vehicle frames has included such notables as the Morris Traveller and Mosquito bomber. Many things now made from metals were made from Ash: such as harrows and rakes.

In the Iron Age ash was used for building houses and causeways.

An infusion of the bark has been used as a cure for

fever, and in the nineteenth century the dried leaves were used as a tea substitute.

Ash has long been known as the best firewood, seasoned or not, and makes good charcoal.

Sometimes the choice of ash wood was enhanced by strong faith in the evil repelling and protective qualities of the tree. A shepherd's crook and the handles of witch's brooms were traditionally made of ash. It was one of the woods for Druids' wands and its roots, which resemble human shapes, like the notorious mandrake plant, were used in magic as healing images.

Present Uses

Ash is in demand by hardwood sawmills and is used for pallets, pulpwood, firewood, tool handles, furniture, and sports equipment (including oars, skis, racquets, and cricket stumps).

Ash is a sought after wood for turnery.

With its clear, pale, glossy finish, it is being increasingly used for high quality furnishings in hotels and public buildings.

Ilex – Holly

Species: *Ilex aquifolium* – holly

Wood Properties

Holly wood is white, hard, dense and very fine-grained.
It distorts when drying, but stains and polishes well.

Past Uses

Holly carves well, and with its hardness has been used for lace bobbins, inlay work, butter-prints, engravers' blocks, chessmen, harpsichord jacks, net-makers' needles and whip stocks.

The bark was boiled and fermented to make birdlime – a sticky substance used to trap small birds which were then eaten. This practice still occurs in some countries in Europe.

Holly has been used for centuries as a decoration at Christmas time. The origin has been traced to the Druids, who decorated their huts with evergreens during winter as an abode for the sylvan spirits, holly (and ivy) being one of the few evergreens available.

Present Uses

The main use for holly these days is for intricate inlay work on decorated furniture.

Holly is also acceptable to wood-engravers as a substitute for box (*Buxus sempervirens*).

Juniperus – Juniper

Species: *Juniperus communis* – juniper

Wood Properties

Juniper is a brown, slow-growing wood that burns with almost no smoke.

Past Uses

There is little evidence of juniper wood being used in products other than carving and turnery.

It was traditionally burnt to smoke and preserve hams, and used to fuel illicit stills in Scotland since little smoke was produced.

Juniper was formerly used to make gunpowder charcoal in the Lake District.

The foliage was good for kindling and the roots were used for basket-making in the Highlands.

Juniper berries have a sharp tang and were used to make liqueurs, counter-poisons (antidotes), and to give gin its flavour. The berries were also used to make a brown dye, and ground for use as a coffee substitute.

The oil from the berries was once used to make varnish, and the seeds were ground to make a peppery sauce.

Present Uses

Juniper is still used to give gin its flavour and make other liqueurs.

Oil of juniper is still available as a cure for flatulence.

Malus – Apple

Species: *Malus sylvestris* – crab apple

Wood Properties

Crab apple wood is very hard with a fine texture. It is pale with darker heartwood.

Past Uses

Apple was sought after for delicate woodworking – once also used for making set squares and other drawing instruments.

With its hardness apple was sometimes used for the cog teeth in water and wind mills.

The apples provided pectin for setting jellies such as rowan or hawthorn. They were also used to make jams and wines and a fermented juice – 'verjuice' – which was a remedy for scalds and sprains.

Apple wood is a good fuel.

Present Uses

There is a small demand for crab apple wood for turning, carving, and furniture-making.

Crab apple pectin is still useful for making jams of fruit low in natural pectin such as strawberries. Apparently pectin can also protect the body against radiation.

An edible oil can be obtained from the seed. But it

would only really be viable to use these seeds as an oil source if the fruit was being used for some purpose such as making cider and then the seeds could be extracted from the remaining pulp

Pinus – Pine

Species: *Pinus sylvestris* – Scots pine

Wood Properties

Scots pine is one of the strongest softwoods. It is resinous and a pale reddish brown, the timber having various common names including red deal, yellow deal and redwood. It can easily be treated (with creosote for example) for outside use, and lasts well in wet conditions.

Past Uses

Large pine poles have been used for ships' masts, telegraph poles, pit props, rafters, railway sleepers, water wheels and water pipes.

It burns well – pine splits used to be used for household lighting, or larger pieces for flaming torches.

Scots pine is said to have been planted in the south of England to mark droveways in snowy weather.

The resin was tapped to produce turpentine (this is still practised on other pine species outside the UK). Pitch, tars and resin can also be obtained from the wood. The tars and oils of turpentine are used in the production of paints and varnishes.

The resin is the base for the production of rosin which

is used for paper sizing, adhesives, inks, and for the maintenance of musical instruments.

Due to its ability to stand wet conditions pine trunks were bored to be used as pipes for domestic water supply in the 18th century.

Shredded pinewood could be woven together to make into rough but strong ropes.

Pine pillows were made, full of the needles or shavings, and were slept on to cure coughs. Pine needles may also have been used in place of hops in early Scottish ale recipes

Present Uses

Scots pine has many commercial uses these days including: fencing, joinery, construction, flooring, packaging, pallets, fibreboard, chipboard, and paper pulp.

The attractive knots in pine make it a sought after timber for furniture making.

It is still sometimes used for railway sleepers and telegraph poles.

Scots pines are occasionally used as Christmas trees.

Essential oil extracted from the needles may be taken for asthma, bronchitis and other respiratory infections, and for digestive disorders such as wind.

Populus – Poplar

Species: *Populus nigra betulifolia* – black poplar
      Populus tremula – aspen

Wood Properties

Poplar wood is lightweight, but absorbs shock well and resists splintering. It is almost white in colour and burns very slowly.

Past Uses

Poplar has been used to make shields, line the bottom of carts, and to make lightweight baskets for fruit and vegetables.

With its low flammability it was used for the floors of oast houses (where hops are dried in beer-making and heat is produced) to reduce the risk of fire. Poplar is also the best wood for matches due to its slow burn.

More recently it has been used for artificial limbs, shelving and packing cases for wine.

Poplar bark was occasionally used for tanning.

Present Uses

There is generally a poor market for poplar wood, but it is sometimes used for veneers, plywood, turnery, and matches.

Prunus - Cherry

Species: *Prunus avium* – wild cherry or gean
         Prunus padus – bird cherry

Wood Properties

Cherry wood is of moderate strength and is reddish brown streaked with gold and pale green. It has a fine, attractive grain and polishes well. It also burns well with a perfumed smoke.

Past Uses

Cherry was prized for making furniture and musical instruments, and for carving and turning.

It was also sometimes used to make cask hoops and was traditionally the wood used for smokers' pipes.

The fruits, particularly of *Prunus avium* (*Prunus padus* cherries being too sour), were a food crop, with branches of wild cherries sold in London streets.

The fruits have also been used in syrups and cough mixtures.

Present Uses

Cherry wood is still sought after for cabinets, turnery and other furniture.

It is also used for veneers, joinery and decorative panelling.

Quercus – Oak

Species: *Quercus petraea* – sessile or durmast oak
Quercus robur – common or pedunculate oak

Wood Properties

The most widely-used hardwood in the UK, oak is hard, strong, resistant to decay and bends well. It is durable and has an even grain.

Past Uses

Although perhaps most famous for its use in shipbuilding, some of the other traditional uses of oak include the following: structural building, pitwood, sea defences, gates, cross bars of telegraph poles, roof tiles, ladder rungs, wheel spokes, furniture, malting vats and wash tubs.

The panelling in the House of Commons is oak.

Oak makes a good charcoal for providing sustained heat and was vital to the iron masters in the making of wrought and cast iron. So much was used that in 1558 a law was passed prohibiting the felling of oak for charcoal in the fear that the naval shipwrights would run out of timber.

It was used to make barrel staves to impart a tannin (or 'oaky') flavour to beers, wines and spirits.

Other uses of oak from the past were the fighting clubs of ancient man, the hammers and long boats of the Vikings, and hafts for daggers and knives were made from its roots.

Oak can be coppiced and was used to make baskets and to provide a regular supply of bark for tanning. It was very important in the leather industry, and vast amounts of bark were used until 1880 when an increasing amount of vegetable tanstuffs was imported. The bark was traditionally stripped in April, May and June; ten tonnes of bark produced one tonne of tannin which treated two tonnes of skins.

Oak acorns were used as an animal fodder, and eaten by humans in times of famine. They could also be roasted as a substitute for almonds and coffee.

Coffins were sometimes made of oak by using large sections of the trunk which were split lengthwise and hollowed out to contain the body. This was only done for state funerals or people of great stature and importance. The shrine of Edward the Confessor in Westminster Abbey is made of marble, but the tomb-chest or coffin beneath (circa 1510) is made of oak, surviving 500 years.

As an emblem of Britain a spray of oak was engraved on the sides of our old sixpence and shilling coins.

Present Uses

Oak is still an important constructional wood, and occasionally used for boat building.

It is also used for structural restoration work, coffins,

quality furniture, veneers, beams, flooring, pulpwood, firewood, fencing and gates.

Although on a reduced scale, it is still used for tanning high quality leathers, and for making barrel staves.

Salix – Willow

Species: *Salix alba* – white willow
   Salix caprea – goat willow or pussy willow
   Salix cinerea – grey willow
   Salix fragilis – crack willow
   Salix pentandra – bay willow
   (*Salix viminalis* – common osier – although not large enough to qualify as a tree this is the most important willow in the basketry industry)

Wood Properties

The wood is light, soft, and resistant to shock, but as far as the majority of its uses are concerned the most important properties of willow are the ability of the stems to bend  without breaking, and its fast growth and ease of vegetative propagation.

Past Uses

Basketry has been a widespread craft in the UK ever since the Celts passed their skills to the Romans. Trimmed willow stems pushed into the ground easily root and grow quickly, and when harvested the one-year-old stems, or 'withies', are woven into a wide range of products including: baskets, hampers, furniture, lobster and crab pots, eel traps, hurdles and so on. When cut to the ground willow coppices produce a crop of withies year after year.

Left to grow larger, willow branches were cut into slats which were interwoven and covered in animal hide to make coracles. These were lightweight boats with a shallow draught that could also be carried by one man across dry or boggy areas. They were first used by the Ancient Britons and are often associated with Wales, although they were also in much use in the Fens by Queen Boadicea's followers.

Willow is also well-known as the wood of cricket bats – cricket was first played in the fourteenth century with the bats cut from any native willow.

Other traditional uses for the wood have been artificial limbs, chip baskets and fruit punnets, toys, cart brake-blocks and flooring, milk pails and milkmaids' yokes.

Thin withies (young stems) have also been used as string for tying faggots or bundles of plants in nurseries.

Willow produces the preferred medicinal charcoal as it contains no harmful residues. The charcoal is very absorbent and has been used for dressing wounds and internally removing toxins including drugs such as aspirin and barbiturates (if taken in excess as an overdose).

Crack willow (*Salix fragilis*) roots were boiled to produce a purple dye which was used to decorate hens' eggs at Easter.

Willow down – the feathery seed covering – was occasionally used for stuffing mattresses.

Present Uses

There is still a small craft industry and revival of interest in basketry.

Cricket bat production is confined to Essex and Suffolk these days, where the variety *Salix alba coerulea* is grown for its straight grain. Ten year-old trees are harvested to make 24 – 32 bats per tree.

A new technique of bioengineering involves erecting two woven hurdles of live willow, the gap between being filled with earth. The willow grows and makes an excellent sound barrier for blocking noise and air pollution from traffic.

Willow is also useful for soil consolidation, windbreaks, and for living garden constructions that take root.

Beds of willow are being tested as a final purification for treated sewage before the cleaned water is returned to rivers.

Finally, there is growing interest in biomass production of willow as a fuel. Coppices can be cut on a 3 – 4 year cycle to produce wood chips that burn cleanly with little ash but producing great heat. The carbon dioxide released into the atmosphere on burning is less than that absorbed by the growing willow – thus combating global warming. In Sweden willow has largely replaced oil as a fuel for industry and domestic heating, and in Denmark a carbon tax has been introduced to reduce carbon emissions and encourage farmers to take up willow growing as an alternative income. In the Fens 25 hectares of willow beds have been planted in an effort to introduce the benefits to the UK.

Sorbus – Rowan, Whitebeam, Service

Species: *Sorbus aria* – whitebeam
Sorbus aucuparia – rowan or mountain ash
Sorbus torminalis – wild service

Wood Properties

Sorbus wood is tough, strong, fine grained, and coloured white to yellow grey. It turns and engraves well.

Past Uses

Sorbus wood has been used for making tool handles, cart wheels, cog wheels, pulleys, gun stocks, and general joinery work.

Rowan wood was sometimes used as a replacement for yew in longbows, and was also made into hoops, baskets and crates.

Whitebeam wood was additionally used to make knife handles, spoons, and billiard cues.

The berries of rowan were made into jelly; but although the whitebeam produces edible berries in autumn, they have a disappointing taste.

The wild service also produces edible berries in autumn and these are very sweet. They were used as a prehistoric equivalent of sugar, and used in brewing to produce chequerberry beer (it was sometimes known as the chequers tree).

Rowan trees were said to guard against the evil effects of 'black' witchcraft. Berries were sometimes strung like beads and hung as a necklace around the neck of a supposed victim of sorcery. Corpses prior to burial and coffins in transit to graveyards were often placed under Rowan trees to protect the souls from evil spirits.

Present Uses

Sorbus woods are rarely used these days, although they are still valued for turnery and engraving.

Rowan berries are still made into jelly on a small scale – usually mixed with equal proportions of crab apples to add pectin, acidity and flavour. This is a traditional accompaniment to cold meat.

You can also try squeezing some fresh rowan berry juice into a gin and tonic - it makes a convincing alternative to Angostura bitters.

Rowan is now a much sought-after wood by those who currently engage in magickal practices (an alternative term for *magic* that was coined to differentiate "the true science of the Magi from all its counterfeits". In the broadest sense, magick is any act performed in order to cause intentional change). Rowan is thought by many to be the preferred wood for making wands and amulets.

Taxus – Yew

Species: *Taxus baccata* – yew

Wood Properties

Yew wood is hard and heavy but elastic. It is a dark reddish brown with a twisted grain and polishes well.

Past Uses

Yew was the best wood for making longbows and spears as it would bend without snapping. In England, Edward III made it compulsory for every able-bodied man to practice archery. This degree led to a huge demand for the wood, which could not be satisfied by home grown Yew. Parliament decreed in 1492 that every ship landing in an English harbour had to bring at least 4 yew bows per ton of freight to remedy this situation.

It was also used traditionally for: barrel hoops, whip stocks, small tool handles, mill cogs, axles and wheels, the bodies of lutes, drinking tankards, parquet floors and long-lasting fence posts.

Present Uses

Today the wood is scarce, but popular with furniture makers. It is also favoured for sculpting, turning and veneers for ornamental work.

There are two chemotherapy drugs that were originally developed from yew trees. One of them, docetaxel, was first made from the needles of the yew tree. It can also be made synthetically, but the needles are still collected and used in the manufacture of the drug. The collecting season tends to be July to September.

Tilia – Lime

Species: *Tilia cordata* – small-leaved lime
         Tilia platyphyllos – large-leaved lime

Wood Properties

Lime wood is soft and pale, good for carving and doesn't warp. It was known by the Romans as 'the tree of a thousand uses'.

Past Uses

Lime is perhaps best known as a carvers' wood. It has been used for many of the great carvings in churches, cathedrals and mansions.

Among its many other uses it was used to make dug-out canoes, agricultural implements, shields, toys, pill-boxes, hat blocks, bobbins, beehive frames, and piano sound-boards and keys.

As it does not taint lime was used for dairy and domestic utensils.

It was also used for glovers' and cobblers' cutting blocks as it does not blunt knives.

Lime makes a very good charcoal which was used to make gunpowder and artists' crayons. The charcoal was also taken by colliers to cure flatulence.

The underbark, or 'bast', was soaked, fermented and beaten to produce coarse fibres which were used to make strong ropes, fishing nets, rough clothing and besom ties. The inner bark was also made into a hot infusion to counteract diarrhoea.

Fibres from the bark of lime trees can also be used for making paper. The stems are harvested in spring or summer, the leaves are removed and the stems steamed until the fibres can be stripped. The outer bark is then removed from the inner bark by peeling or scraping. The fibres are cooked for two hours with lye and then beaten in a ball mill. The resulting paper is beige in colour.

Lime flowers were used to make a summer tea, and the leaves were even occasionally eaten in sandwiches.

A chocolate substitute can be made from a paste of the ground-up flowers and immature fruit.

Present Uses

Lime wood is mostly used for turnery and carving these days.

It is still sometimes used for piano parts, other musical instruments and when making wooden beehives.

Lime flower tea is used internally in the treatment of indigestion, hypertension, hardening of the arteries, hysteria, nervous vomiting or palpitation. The flowers are harvested commercially and often sold in health shops.

Beekeepers regard lime trees as a good source of nectar.

Ulmus – Elm

Species: *Ulmus carpinifolia* – smooth-leaved elm (possibly a very early introduction rather than truly native)

> *Ulmus glabra* – wych elm
> *Ulmus procera* – English elm

Wood Properties

Elm is a tough wood, rosy brown in colour, that is difficult to split although it distorts easily and needs careful seasoning. It is durable in wet conditions.

Past Uses

Its durability in water has led elm to be used for water pipes, watermill wheel blades, paddle-steamer blades, battleship keels, underwater works at docks and harbours, pump buckets and boat building.

Elm wood has also been used to make: kitchen chair seats, weather-boarding for farm buildings, garden furniture, mangers, wheel hubs, bowls, egg cups, candlesticks, cheese moulds, bellow-backs, coffins, furniture and turnery.

When used to make medicinal charcoal in ancient times, a decoction of the bark in water was favoured by the charcoal burners to bathe burns. The bark was also used in medicines to treat broken bones, gout and dropsy.

The tough inner bark was sometimes used as a source of fibres for mats and ropes, and, as it is rich in starch, was prepared as a gruel and eaten by the charcoal burners.

For thousands of years, people collected elm leaves to feed to their cattle. It is believed that an over-harvesting of elm leaves caused a decline in the trees about five thousand years ago. Elm leaves were still fed to cattle, up until the 10th century, and it is still used for this purpose in other countries.

In Scotland wych elm is the more common species. In Gaelic it is known as 'leven', as in Loch Leven in Kinross, and was often used in the dyeing of wool. An early form of tie-dyeing was used to create intermittent colours in woollen. Twine made from the inner bark of the elm tied tightly at regular intervals, to form 'hanks' of the yarn, was used to stop a dye from reaching the wool.

Present Uses

With the massive decline in the number of elm trees in the UK, due to Dutch elm disease, the wood is now rarely used. In the last hundred years the disease has killed millions of elm trees and changed the British landscape.

Dutch elm disease is caused by a fungus, which is spread by the elm bark-beetle. The beetle eats its way through bark, and the fungus is left behind inside the tree. The beetle also lays eggs inside the elm tree, which hatch into burrowing larvae. It seems that the beetles only seek trees over a certain size to lay their eggs, which is why there are still elm hedges and saplings throughout the country.

Old elm is still prized for turnery and, when available, also used for veneers.

Further Resources

The Arboricultural Association – Setting the standard for arboriculture in the UK, Ireland and beyond. 2000 members practising arboriculture as consultants, government officers, contractors ('tree surgeons'), lecturers, researchers and students. Main activities include

- setting standards in arboricultural contracting, consulting and local government tree management
- helping people meet those standards by publishing information and providing training through workshops, conferences, the Arborists' Trade Fair and academic qualifications
- promoting competent arboriculturists and proper tree care to practitioners and society.

Arboricultural Association
Ampfield House, Ampfield, Romsey, Hants SO51 9PA
Tel +44 (0) 1794 368717; Fax +44 (0) 1794 368978
Email admin@trees.org.uk Web www.trees.org.uk

The Association of Polelathe Turners and Greenwood Workers was created in 1990 by a group of a dozen like minded individuals who wanted to rescue the art of polelathe turning and greenwood working from obscurity. Fifteen years on and the organisation has a global membership of over 500.
Web: www.bodgers.org.uk

The **British Trees** website aims to be the definitive guide to British tree species on the Internet and was kindly donated to the Woodland Trust by Bill Unsworth in 2004. Web: www.british-trees.com

Common Ground is internationally recognised for playing a unique role in the arts and environmental fields, distinguished by the linking of nature with culture, focussing upon the positive investment people can make in their own localities, championing popular democratic involvement, and by inspiring celebration as a starting point for action to improve the quality of our everyday places. Common Ground offers ideas, information and inspiration through publications and projects such as Parish Maps, Apple Day, Community Orchards, Tree Dressing Day, Confluence and the campaign for Local Distinctiveness.

Common Ground, Gold Hill House, 21 High Street, Shaftesbury, Dorset SP7 8JE
Tel: 01747 850820
Email: info@commonground.org.uk
Web: www.commonground.org.uk

Country Smallholding is a practical monthly magazine, for smallholders new and old and anyone with an interest in keeping livestock, growing, organics, the environment, self-sufficiency, and everything related to small scale farming and the Good Life, both in the country and in town. For more information see www.countrysmallholding.com or contact the editor on 01392 888481

The Dendrologist was established in 1983 for the benefit of all those individuals and groups in the Chilterns area who wish to take an informed interest in a wide range of aspects of trees and woodlands, including their management. As its reputation spread so did its popularity and it's now sent quarterly to readers throughout Britain for an annual subscription of £7.50. It is still researched, written and produced by volunteers for what is effectively a federation of tree interested people, bringing them together to share events, news and information about trees and also their management and care.
Web: www.treematters.freeserve.co.uk

Eco Tree Care & Conservation is a co-operative of arborists and woodsmen in Hertfordshire. We approach arboriculture and business with as much environmental and social integrity as possible. Everyday services are tree surgery, tree planting, native hedge planting and woodland management. We are actively recycling our waste, exploring sustainable energy solutions, promoting sustainable woodland management and promoting good tree surgery. A high profile web presence has become a resource for information on arboriculture and woodland management and for those wishing to pursue a career with trees – Our philosophy *"We must be the change we wish to see in the world"*

Eco Tree Care & Conservation
Tel: 01920 420142 / 07725 583201
Email: martin@ecotreecare.co.uk
Web: www.ecotreecare.co.uk

The Forestry & Timber Association is the leading representative body for all those involved in the growing, tending, harvesting and management of trees, throughout the UK. FTA engages with government and non-government organisations to represent members' interests through political and technical representation. FTA supports strategic market development; seeks to improve industry competitiveness; and promotes economic and business development, including training support. Membership is open to anyone engaged or interested in forestry, woodlands or trees, whether for commercial, amenity or other reasons.

The Forestry & Timber Association
5 Dublin Street Lane South Edinburgh EH1 3PX
Tel: 0131 538 7111
Email: info@forestryandtimber.org
Web: www.forestryandtimber.org

Forests Forever is the environmental voice of the timber industry and aims to promote the environmental benefits of timber as well as encourage environmentally responsible trading practices. It offers advice and information to the Government, other organisations and its Members on how to source timber and timber products responsibly.
Web: www.forestsforever.org.uk

The International Society of Arboriculture (ISA) is the worlds biggest group of professional arborists with over 14,000 members distributed throughout 38 "chapters" across the 5 continents. The ISA operates in the United Kingdom & Ireland via it's UK&I Chapter. The Chapter formed in 1992 to represent the UK based professional arborist and to promote an international platform for the advancement of the science of arboriculture.
Web: www.isa-uki.org

For over 80 years **International Tree Foundation** has been planting trees in the UK and overseas, following in the footsteps of our founder, Richard St Barbe Baker. St Barbe himself is believed to have been instrumental in the planting of 26 trillion trees, through organisations he founded or helped. Today ITF continues his vision- planting trees that work for communities throughout the world. If you would like to help us in this work please contact; info@internationaltreefoundation.org , write to us at:

International Tree Foundation, Sandy Lane, Crawley Down, West Sussex, RH10 4HS.
Or phone on 0870-7744269
Web: www.internationaltreefoundation.org

The **Small Woods Association** is Britain's leading organisation in supporting and promoting the work done by the owners and carers of small woodlands. Courses, information and networking – a must for anyone who owns a small wood. Provides access to a low cost public liability insurance scheme.
Tel 01743 792644 enquiries@smallwoods.org.uk

Now includes the Green Wood Centre www.greenwoodcentre.org.uk tasked by Forestry Commission with leading the revival in coppice and greenwood crafts.
Web: www.smallwoods.org.uk

Stovesonline are a nationwide supplier of wood burning and multifuel stoves, flue pipe, flue liner and everything you need to install a stove or build a chimney. www.stovesonline.co.uk has lots of advice about stoves, chimneys, installation techniques, regulations, common problems. There is a wide range of stoves to choose from and a searchable database of stove installers, fuel suppliers and chimney sweeps. Stovesonline offer a free installation design service – given a few details experts will design a regs. compliant installation and then liaise with your installer. Stovesonline deal with architects, contractors and domestic clients in the UK and Europe.
Tel: 0845 226 5754
Email: info@stovesonline.co.uk
Web: www.stovesonline.co.uk

The-Tree is a non-profit website dedicated to sharing information about the many different facets of knowledge about trees and forests: Excellent section on British Trees, Trees and the Environment, Cultivation, Tree Medicine, Permaculture and Agroforestry, Woodcrafts, Myths and Folklore, Philosophy, Customs and Culture inspired by trees, Forest news.
Web: www.the-tree.org.uk

Environmental charity **The Tree Council** is a partnership of 150 organisations working together for trees. It also co-ordinates the national volunteer Tree Warden Scheme. The Tree Council works for effective action for trees, more trees, of the right kind, in the right places, and better care for all trees of all ages. To help achieve its goal of making trees matter to everyone, it organises an annual programme of public involvement initiatives which includes National Tree Week. It also includes Seed Gathering Season, a time to make the most of trees for their autumn colours and the seeds, nuts and fruits that they produce.

Further information from www.treecouncil.org.uk
The Tree Council
71 Newcomen Street, London SE1 1YT

Trees For Life: Moved by the plight of the ancient Caledonian Forest which by the end of the late 20th century was only a fragmented 1% of its original 1.5 million hectares, consisting of scattered remnants of old trees nearing the end of their lives and with over grazing by deer preventing natural regeneration, Trees for Life began work in 1989 to help regenerate and expand the forest. Now Trees for Life is the only organisation working for the restoration of the Caledonian and all of its constituent species to a large contiguous area in the Highlands of Scotland. They have planted over half a million native trees, created enclosures, removed non-native species and are unique in combining an inspiring vision with practical action on the ground.

Trees for Life, The Park, Finhorn Bay, Forres, Moray, IV36 3TU Scotland.
Tel: 0845 458 3505
Web: www.treesforlife.org.uk

Treesource – *Supporting Professional Arborists*
Treesource book shop brings together a ready source of topical and essential reference works for the tree professional. This mail order book shop offers a diverse range of tree books of use to tree professionals in the course of their work and continues to source new material as well as providing arborists with regular book news and updates. Treesource also publishes the *Tree Sourcebook*, a directory of arboricultural contacts and resources. This is an essential reference tool for anyone working with trees, including local authority tree officers, contractors, consultants and service providers. Tel/Fax: 01904 720126
Email: info@treesource.co.uk
Web: www.treesource.co.uk

The Woodland Trust is the UK's leading woodland conservation charity. Since its foundation in 1972, it has been protecting and caring for native woodland. The Trust achieves its aims through a combination of acquiring woodland and sites for planting, advocacy of the importance of conserving ancient woodland and highlighting its place in the wider environment, caring for woodland wildlife and enhancing biodiversity, creation of new woods, and increasing enjoyment of woodland through public access and inspiring projects. For more information, please telephone 01476 581135 or visit:

Web: www.woodland-trust.org.uk

Lightning Source UK Ltd.
Milton Keynes UK
UKOW052359061211

183261UK00002BA/1/A